Morton W. Spencer

The Rosy Cross

Morton W. Spencer

The Rosy Cross

ISBN/EAN: 9783337254087

Printed in Europe, USA, Canada, Australia, Japan

Cover: Foto ©Lupo / pixelio.de

More available books at **www.hansebooks.com**

THE ROSY CROSS;

OR,

CHRIST IN THE CATACOMBS.

A POEM,

BY

MORTON W. SPENCER, A.M.

BUFFALO:
BIGELOW BROTHERS, STEAM PRINTERS.
Cor. Seneca and Pearl Streets.
1880.

Entered according to Act of Congress, in the year 1880, by
MORTON W. SPENCER,
In the Office of the Librarian of Congress at Washington.
All rights reserved.

THIS POEM

IS

RESPECTFULLY DEDICATED

TO

YOUNG DISCIPLES OF CHRIST.

"Rex tremendæ majestatis,
Qui salvandus salvas gratis,
Salva me, fons pietatis.

Seria contritione,
Gratiæ apprehensione,
Vitæ emendatione.

Quando cœli sunt movendi,
Dies adsunt tunc tremendi,
Nullum tempus pœnitendi.

O tu Deus majestatis,
Alme candor trinitatis,
Nunc conjunge cum beatis."

CONTENTS.

Chapter.		Page.
I.	The Catacombs,	7
II.	The Martyrs,	19
III.	Discourse—Creation,	31
IV.	Trial of Faith,	42
V.	Pagan Deities,	51
VI.	Incidents,	61
VII.	Claudia,	76
VIII.	Rome,	93
IX.	The Coming of Christ,	106
X.	The Final Triumph,	121
	Notes,	135

ILLUSTRATIONS.

		Page.
I.	Portrait of the Author,	
II.	The Appian Way,	11
III.	The Plan of the Catacombs,	22
IV.	Inscriptions,	45
V.	The Fossor,	66
VI.	The Secret Stairs,	87
VII.	The City of Rome,	95

ARGUMENT:

The scene of the following poem is laid chiefly in and under the City of Rome, Italy. It is designed to illustrate the special Divine care of the Church of Jesus Christ in the first centuries.

THE ROSY CROSS.

CHAPTER I.

THE CATACOMBS.

Day glimmers in the East. The sky,
In Indian Summer tints, and high
In Heaven the fair white Moon is hung,
Which on our devious path has flung
From beaming face a friendly ray.
While far adown the Appian Way,
We wander 'mid the types of power—
The obelisk, and arch, and tower,
Or stately tombs with ruins wild,
Moss-clung; where from the marble piled,
Antique in beauty, is forecast
A shadow from the buried past.

The skirtings of Imperial Rome
On either side,—a villa home

Rises distinctly to the view,
Of various and changeful hue;
Whose inmates were perhaps, in fine,
Extracted from some noble line
Of Romans of Prætorian birth,
Of ancestorial wealth and worth.
There, too, the Mausolea stand
Moldering; yet, in their ruins, grand,
A wreck upon the rolling main
Of verdure, stranded on the plain.
And, too, crowning the summit swells—
Girt with the wide, deep, woodland dells—
Stately Basilicas uprise,
Seeming to part the floating skies;
Beneath whose walls the mighty dead
Recline,—chieftains, and heroes led
By fiery ambition, on
To deeds of darkness,—and anon
You read their tablets; poor renown
Is the World's look of praise, or frown!

Not warriors of the world alone,
Contending for the glittering throne,—

The final, grand, triumphal hour,
The crown, the scepter, and the power;
Not these, the heroes we shall bring,
Be ours a humbler theme to sing;—
The noble host of martyred slain,
Their smile at death, their piercing pain,
Their throne, their crown, their sceptered
    power:
And when the grand triumphal hour
Shall come, at Resurrection morn,
The trophies which their lives adorn.

In the Dark Days,—at midnight hour,
When Persecution's awful power
Raged like a lion, fierce and bold,
And wealth and beauty, young and old,
Fled to the mountains far, and found
Refuge in clefted rocks profound.
Methinks that Satan's wily wrath,
Tracing the long and bloody path,
Must tire at length, and find relief
From the great burden of his grief;
For now a Mightier Power withholds

The direful stroke, whose arm controls
This faint expression of his ire,—
The rack, and chain, and sword, and fire.

Outside the limit-walls that day,—
More than a league, it seemed, away,
We sought adown that "Queen of roads,"
Those subterranean abodes
Where Christians long were wont to live,
And on their sacred altars give
Earth's comforts. Tangled vines surround
Their entrance; beneath, are found
Large excavations, caverns deep:
We grope along the rugged steep,
A narrow way, and damp as death,—
Renew instinctively our breath;
Then lights, for we are not misled,
Stream through the darkness just ahead,
Enter the low and narrow door
And blaze the gray old tufa floor:
When lo! the gloomy walls expand
Into a stately arch and grand,
Now here, now there, diversified

THE APPIAN WAY.

We sought adown that "Queen of Roads,"
Those subterranean abodes
Where Christians long were wont to live.—Page 10.

With gems of art on every side.

A temple—hewed in solid rock,
So worshipful; here, where the flock
Of Christ gathered in other days,
Were wont to hymn sublimest praise.
Saints in these caverns silent slept,
The faithful here in anguish wept,—
And here rejoiced that for his name
Were counted worthy of the shame.
Oh midnight horror! Shall it reign
Like night in depths of ocean main
Forever? Shall there come a day
To scatter such dense clouds away?
Some marble steps before the door,
Your entrance within entice;
Mosaics decorate the floor,
Of delicate and strange device;
The walls covered with stucco white,
Or pigment red, with beauty bright;
Semi-detached, firm pillars stand—
Cut in volcanic rock. The hand
Of Art alone had chiseled deep

Cornice and capital, which keep
Their proud position in the nooks,
Where each on each his fellow looks:
Niches, at the angles of the walls,
Are cleft for lamps which light these halls;
A strong and arching roof, sky-lit,
Few struggling rays of light admit:
Four pillars from their sockets rise
Near to the walls, sufficient size
For table bases,—doubtless, where
Were taken sacraments with prayer;
Around which, lattice work is wrought;
'Twas here the sacred teacher taught.

Stay, and one curious thought bestow,—
On every side, above, below,
Are subterranean chambers, strewed
In groups, which were in darkness hewed;
Tier above tier, room after room,
And each a martyr's royal tomb:
These faced with blocks of marble, all
Elaborately carved to taste,
Present in this sepulchral hall,

Inscriptions elegant and chaste;
In gilded urns their ashes rest,
Their names in fragrant memory blest.
Here the Sarcophagi,—deep cut
In solid marble, long-while shut
And sealed against the elements,
Sunk in the pavement. Sentiments
Of filial love and pious care,
Adorn these tombs—rich, old and rare.

Deep in these crypts, Pastors of Rome
And worthies, found a quiet home,—
Who gently dropped this mortal frail.
Unto our view the heavens unveil
A glorious army! what can add
To them of joy, in white robes clad!
Art-gems, set in these secret walls,
Their portraiture adorns these halls.
Here, they in priestly robes, the grand
Insignia of their office, stand;
Wearing the stole and tonsure bright,
And nimbus, dazzling to the sight!
O wondrous City of the Dead,

Whose sepulchers have not misled
The lowly pilgrim at the shrine
Of saints; caverns where lamp lights shine,
And where the ardent fires aglow
Upon the hearth, their warmth bestow.

A time of worship,—lamps were hung
And on the congregation flung
Their mellow light, and torches flamed
Along the labyrinths; men came
And bowed them there, not to be seen
Of men, hushed in the pure serene
Of worship that subdues the heart.
Fountains unseal, that there impart
Health to the multitudes who bowed
Their heads, when something like a cloud
Of flaming glory o'er them hung,
And on them heavenly fragrance flung.

One was their glorious Lord; their vows
Richly, his grace and strength endows·
One Fatherhood in God above,—
One bond of unity in Love;

One brotherhood in Christ the Son,
Whose Church in heaven and earth is one,
One Spirit, by whose mighty power
They stand; their Bulwark and their Tower.
One spirit fallen, now reborn;
One glorious Resurrection morn:
At one Baptismal scene they stand
In fellowship of heart and hand.
Out of one Gospel Mint are coined,
All hearts in one Communion joined.
One faith, one hope, one joy, one strife,
One Head, one Truth, one Way, one Life.
One Kingdom's universal reign,
One vast Eternity sublime;
One Hell to shun, one Heaven to gain,
And only one probation time.

Low bowing, as their hearts prepare
Their lips to utter words in prayer:—

Oh Thou, to whom night is as day,
Look on our darkness, and survey
These sorrows and our mighty woe!

Look, and thy strengthening Grace bestow;
Behold, O God our Shield, to Thee
We hasten with the Beggar's plea.
Father, forgive those tyrants bold,
To their dark minds thy truth unfold
Who trample down the streets of Rome
The blood of innocence, many a home
To execution given—set forth to wait
The day of slaughter—desolate.
Yet, Elder Brother, through a sense
Of tender care and providence,
Lifting the hand, the feeble knee,—
We stay our fainting hearts on Thee.
Forgive, and let us find that place
Hid by the shadows of thy Grace.

Omnific Word! whose thorn-pierced brow
A crown Divine in glory now
Adorns; whose portrait on these walls
We often traced, stone-cut in halls
Or tablet-aisles. Thee, we adore!
Whose tender love our burdens bore.
Transfused in Thee the Father shines,

Whose full-orbed countenance enshrines
So much of Heaven, pity and power,
Thy life fragrant as summer flower.
With joy thy servants own thy sway.
Oh hasten on the glorious day
Foretold and by the Prophets sung.
Yet down through all the ages rung
Let us behold thy Glory, stand
Before Thee and from thy command
Instructed, will go forth to bless.
Great Intercessor! wilt thou press
Our plea before the Father's court,
Our halting steps raise and support,
Safe bring us to to the world above.
Thine be the Heaven, Thine the Love.

I.

Praise ye the Lord, ye heavens above,
And wondrous heights confirm His love.
Ye shining hosts of angels bright,
The sun, the moon, the stars of light,
The floating firmament on high,
And cloud-born waters of the sky.

II.

Praise ye the Lord. At his command,
Created, 'stablished by his hand,—
The verdant valley, rocky steep,
The monsters of the rolling deep,
The fire, the hail, the snow, the cloud,
The stormy winds and thunder loud,

III.

The hills, the snow-capped mountains fair,
The fruitful trees and cedars rare,
The beasts and every creeping thing,
The very birds of every wing;
The proudest king, the people, praise
The Lord our God of Ancient Days.

IV.

Princes and judges of the earth,
Young men and maidens in their mirth,
And little children with their sire,
Praise Him upon the trembling lyre;
His excellence and glory bless,
His people's praise and Righteousness.

Thus worshipful, the service o'er,
These friends of Christ through open door
Retire,—but not to safe repose.
Before another evening's close,
Where tyrants rule, new perils wait;
The terrors of impending hate
May weave a Martyr's Crown for those,
Who triumph in the face of foes.

CHAPTER II.

THE MARTYRS.

A HUNDRED Martyrs at the stake.
A hundred, at the morning's break,
A hundred, light the evening fires—
A hundred on their funeral pyres!
Who died in hope; and yet that day
More luminous than " Milky Way,"
The path they made to glory. There
Long time it grew—the Church of God,
Fast founded on the Ancient Rock,
Marking the steps of Faith they trod.

Each day were multiplied in Rome
Believers, added from the home
Of many of ignoble birth,
Or the dilapidated throne
Of Cæsar's household. Under Rome,
Beneath the Capitoline dome,
They lived and loved, making these rooms
Their home for months, perhaps for years,
Defences from their mortal fears.

The *Luminairi* pour their light
And ventilating air within.
Descending through a stairway flight,
Where the true Catacombs begin,
Are labyrinthine corridors;
Five stories deep our feet were led
Down through the chapels of the dead,
Where long wandered the Confessors.
Five hundred miles these winding ways
Extend! down sombre depths two score,
Perhaps to fifty feet or more—
Where even feeble struggling rays
Come not; where once volcanic fire

Belched from earth's babbling mouth ablaze,
Now cold; *so may the white-heat ire*
Tyrants have kindled for these days,
Irradiate on them in vain
Who wrestled for the faith;—now reign

These sacred chambers, deeply hewed
In the soft porous tufa rock,
Defended long the ancient flock
Of the Messiah. Prayers endued
This consecrated holy place.
Each story had its graven walls,
Each chapel, too, its sacred halls,
Where lived this persecuted race;
Each with the symbols of the past
Adorned: pictures of Prophets cast,
With drapery of sacred scenes
Are here,—where affluence once reigned.
On these dark rocky beds remained
The inspiration of the soul
Of genius, which expressed the goal
Ideal which the life blood warmed.
Records a faith sublime, that wings

Its happy flight the ages through;—
The pure, the beautiful, the true,
The Gospel of Redemption sings.

Tombs of the blessed saints are here,
Held fragrant in our memory;
Their dust, by many a friend and dear,
Is laid in this dark gallery,
Deep excavated in the rocks
Within the walls. On marble blocks
That guard each entrance to the dead,
Deep-cut, some tender words were read.
Engraved beneath a branching palm,
The figure of a dove or lamb,
Beneath the cross, or sacred fish,—
Some slight expression of the wish
Of parting friend or sister dear,
Or mother, is recorded here.

O, wonderful that ancient Art !
That stones deep-cut, unearthed, impart
Such treasures to the curious view—

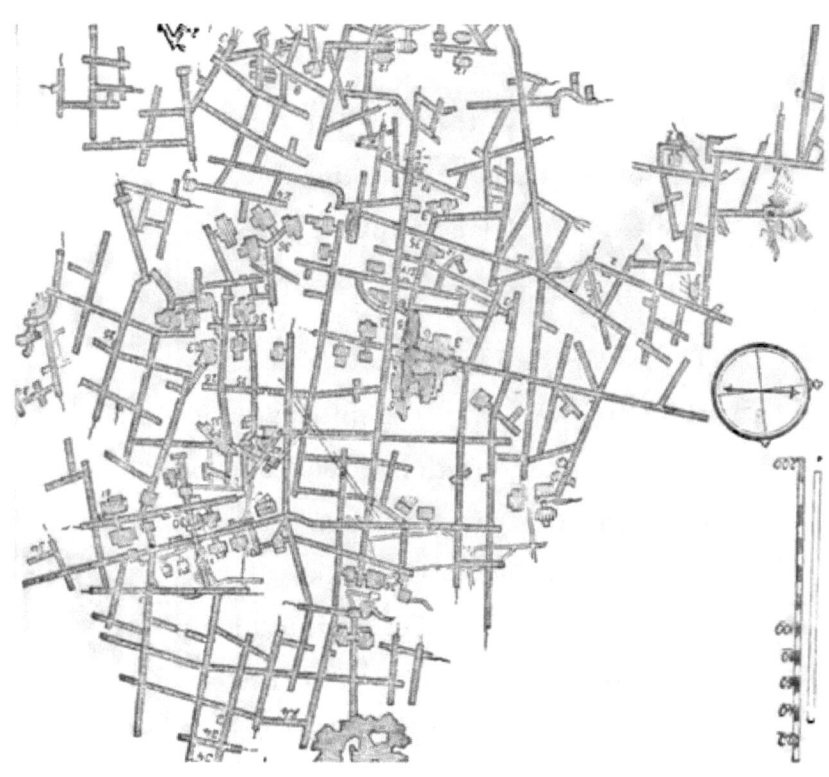

Of dross refined, the tried and true
Of Rome's magnificence; no crown
More dazzling than the Martyrs:—down
Through mighty Cæsar's golden years—
The earth's dread ordeal of tears !
How strange! no grander lives were wrought
With sweeter memories were frought,
For ages yet to be.   Lo ! where
Are now the robes Imperials wore ?
Their gold and purple, stained with crime,
Fringed with the tinsel of their time ?

When twilight deepens down the sky,
The struggling moonbeams, feeble, shy,
Send forth a sympathizing ray
To light poor wanderers on their way—
Who, under cover of the night,
Oft quickly to the markets hie,
Their various needs and wants supply;
With flowing tears that blind the sight,
Oft venture to some cherished spot,
Or threshold of a friendly cot,
Revisiting their former friends

And customed scenes, till nightfall ends;
Friends, neighbors, quickly gather round
Who with God's earthly gifts abound,
Are ready to divide their store
And sympathy and comfort pour.
Regaled by breezes from above,
Refreshed by solaces of love,
They then retire; their simple fare
Each with the other vies to share.

Sometimes in humble garments clad,
By poverty made doubly sad,
They drink from gushing fountains there,
Partake of food that friends prepare.
At times these fugitives are fed
From hidden chambers in the crypts;
Abundant fruits, grains, wines and bread
There stored away, await the hour
Of Persecution's vengeful power.

Yet once, bethink their lowly state!
Ye who with pride of wealth dilate:
The poverty, the pinching want!

Think of the barbed dart, the taunt
Of enemies! behold the face
Pallid with sickness, view the trace
Of beauty, or of strength their own
Once cherished, now forever flown.
O wonderful! the weary eye
To which the glorious sunlit sky
Has seldom come,—perhaps for years
Have full orbed sorrows flowed in tears;
And all because they loved the cross!
They loved the crown as well—the dross
Of worldly pleasure won not; love,
Fast bound them to that Friend above,
Prompted to deeds unselfish, brave,
Unnumbered woes,—their hope, the grave

These soldiers of the hated Cross,
Those who have counted all but dross
To win the knowledge pure, of Him
Who in a rock-ribbed sepulchre
Was laid, are hither brought in dim
Of midnight torch. How oft occur
Such dangers, that the flaming lamp

Extinguished to elude pursuit,
Into the darkness and the damp
Is cast away. Still resolute,
In armor of defences clad,
Bold Roman Guards with frenzy mad
Oft urge the Christians' hasty flight—
Who plunge in intricacies deep,
Or dash resistless out of sight,
And still serene their vigils keep.

Perchance the sweetly solemn lays
Of Christian worship and of praise,
Whose soft and measured cadence steals
Down the long corridors, reveals
Their prey—the soldiery amaze!
Changing the purpose of that hour
With saving sanctifying power.
Not always thus, betrayers bold,
Smit with a Judas' greed for gold,
Surprise them at devotions pure—
Their refuge oft their Sepulture!
Thus while they ministered and prayed,
Such was their fearful tragic fate—

Daily to each new perils wait.
O sad, mid sacred rites and prayers,
The hush of every whispered groan.
Even in caverns deep and lone
That one of this dear life despairs!

Impenetrable gloom! no light
Of day breaks on their customed sight.
Around the Martyr's fiery brand
Were virtues moldering embers fanned;—
Love's inextinguishable flame,
Faith gazing on a burnished name,
Exultant hopes, immortal fame,
And conscience quick—illuminate
Abodes so dark and desolate.
There wit and wisdom oft distill
Through intellect and heart and will.
There Reason's ruddy face is lit,
Her brilliant flashings far remit
The darkness. These were the rays
That wandered through the gloom, the fount
Bubbling hard by from Zion's mount.–
Earth's echoes to remoter days.

Upon the rocks, not soon to fade,
These wonderful inscriptions laid
With mystic Monogram, the sign
Of martyrdom, their names enshrine.
" In peace they sleep; will wake to live
" Forever, and refreshment find.—
" Called hither by the angels.—Gave
" Their blood-stained bodies to the tomb.—
" Their ashes sifted to the wind,
" Their souls sparkle beyond the stars
" In palaces of ample room.—
" Forever dried their weeping eyes.—
" Hushed are their bosoms heaving sighs,
" And their all deathless spirits rest
" Within the holy tents.—The blest,
" The beautiful, the good are there;
" And crowns the conquering heroes wear.
" Hither the legions quick repair.—
" Hail! Farewell. May God refresh thee!
" Have thou a prosperous voyage.—
" Not yet two little years of age,
" May the earth be light upon thee.—

"To a sweet and prattling daughter;
"Good Cheer! quaff the cooling water.—

"Pius, he sleeps among the good.—
"Most chaste and modest wife
"Of wondrous faith; wise, pious, kind,
"My Dear; sweeter than light and life,—
"God's little lamb.—My little dove.—
"O take me to thy self, my Love.—
"Now sleep in peace among the just;
"Farewell. Eternal light to thee.—
"Buried with tears in this damp clay,
"With us, how very short his stay;
"Asleep in Jesus Christ our Lord."

In a few Pagan chambers trace
Inscriptions, and the contrast mark.—
"The cruel fates me snatched away.—
"Fearfully hurried in the dark
"On the unknown infernal bark.
"Close by the river brink; no ray
"Of hope here penetrates the gloom.—
"All that is left to me, this tomb.—

"Dear mother earth once nourished me
"And now receives me to her breast.—
"Neither to you nor yet to me
"Is granted the forever rest.—
"Good cheer! for none immortal are.—
"Living, I lived on sumptuous fare.
"My play is ended now, and soon
"Yours will be, forever; Farewell.—
"All that I ate and drank I have,
"And what besides I left, I lost."

Sweet memories linger, guard each name
These rugged grottoes give to fame;
Of noble deed, and thought, and worth—
The truest noblemen of earth!
Whose lives were the foundation stones
Deep laid, on which proud Rome had stood.
The wise, the pure, the great, the good,
Whose sweat and tears and blood and groans
Are here depicted on the rock,
That guarded once God's ancient flock.

Nor marvel! linger here; why not?
Illustrious labyrinths of death,—

Rather of life, hushed to a breath!
Not here the Christian's lonely lot
Alone inspires; abundant joy—
Written in characters of light,
Embossed with gold without alloy,
And sacred as the robes of white,
Or relics in the sculptured urn,
Earth for a thousand years enjoyed:
Where artists' various skill employed
To make the marble breathe, so rife
With beauty and the glow of life,
Their ardent forms reanimate.
We would admirers, emulate
Their virtues who now sheltered, deep,
Down in the Rock of Ages sleep.

CHAPTER III.

CREATION.

The Pastor of the flock is heard,
Discoursing from the Ancient Word.

Primeval Night—brooded the waste
Of Chaos, and his wings embraced
The farthest bounds of space immense,
Before that burst of radiance
Creation saw;—astonished heard
The fiat of His potent Word—
Who is the Light, Offspring Supreme,
Eternal, Co-eternal Beam.

When first that joyful morning broke,
God *smiled;* the universe awoke!
The empty realms of darkest death
Were moved by his Almighty breath:
From void abyss the orbs of flame
Ten thousand times ten thousand came.

God *spake:* see round the centre roll
A million suns on steady pole;
Afar they dart the kindling ray,
The all-pervading law obey:
The lesser lights pursue their race
New-poised within the void of space,
Each onward move in ample round,
No discord, not one jarring sound.

God's Home on high—His Holy Place,—
Was the grand centre of their race:
Around the High and Holy One—
Whose palace was the central Sun,
Where systems piled on systems, swung—
World after world a myriad hung.
All round their centre, centres roll;
Complete, extended, boundless, whole,
Uncircumscribed and limitless,
They wheel around that realm of bliss
On which His Throne shall stand secure,
Whose might and glory must endure.

The glorious God, *unveiled* his face,
And light o'erflowed unbounded space,

Till worlds had drank the silvery tides
Poured round their ever-blooming sides·
And isles of green and clouds of white
Were bathed in floods of liquid light.
He, from his throne, *put forth* his hand
To fill the sea and pile the land;
He made the mist, the floating cloud,
The lightning, and the thunder loud;
He made the earth all bright and new,
Each herb and tree before it grew—
And ere 'twas in the genial soil,
Or man had learned to till or toil.
He formed each plant and spire of grass,
The verdure of the rolling mass,
The beasts and every creeping thing,
And every bird of every wing:
He blessed, and called them very good,
Living in happy brotherhood.

Just from the hand of God, and fresh,
Two glorious spirits clad in flesh—
Pure as the dew, or fountain jet
Or nectar of the floweret—

Appeared in Eden's lovely bowers:
Adam, with wondrous pristine powers,
Gentle as evening's quiet hush;
And Eve, fair daughter all ablush—
Reflects the rosy from her cheek—
When eye and lip and soul bespeak
The hope, the joy, all graces true
To God, to each,—love's proper hue.
Their lives in holy bonds are wed.
Here nature's choicest dainties spread
A rich repast on velvet blade,
Beneath a dome of pendant shade.

When all the mighty work was done—
World joined to world, and sun to sun—
All beautiful and bright and fair,
Think you the angels were not there?
They seek the presence of their King—
Their offering to his Altar bring;
Robed in the azure of the sky,
The lightning flashing from their eye,
A gorgeous crown their brows embrace,
And with their wings they veil their face;

While in his presence they appear,
O'erawed with glory, not with fear.
They come from far, they wing their flight
Just from the dazzling world of light,
With organs of eternal praise,
To Him enraptured anthems raise.
Creation's joy, their hearts inspire,
Touched by the sacred Heavenly fire
That burns, and bursts, and glows, anew
To God, the High, the Pure, the True.

O when the sons of Heaven of old
Swelled their first praise, or rolled
Their anthems o'er the mighty throng,
Assembled worlds with joyful song
Set to the music of the spheres,
Rolled ever on through endless years.
These sons of God without delay,
Methinks, were quickly on their way
To search the realms from near and far,
And climb the hights from star to star;
Or let their mighty vision sweep
Where space is but the endless deep:

Far in the distance they descry
A little speck—they quickly fly
Descending through the realms of air
To reach the worlds of glory where
A happy sisterhood revolves,
Each planet in the light dissolves.
They pass the stars, they pass the sun,
They pass the moon—their triumph won.
This new-made child of Heavenly birth,
They name it first—*Our Beauteous Earth*.

Mind was of nature all Divine—
Completely made to soar and shine;
To range the beauteous fields of thought
In which God's wondrous hand had wrought.
Earth's Angels, clad in form erect,
Were good, and quick of intellect;
With reason right and heart so pure
That naught within could ere allure
Their feet from paths which virtue trod,
The path of safety and of God.
They loved the beautiful and fair
On land, in sea, and sky and air,

Earth's crystal founts and shady brooks,
Old rock-ribbed haunts and quiet nooks,
Her towering cliffs and lowly vales,
Her lakes and seas, in calms and gales.

To them the flowers their fragrance gave,
For them the mighty forests wave;
To add one joy, the verdant fields
Are spread with all that nature yields.

On every plain, on every hill,
The tides of life in every rill,
Swell and reëcho in each heart,
And joy unspeakable impart.

Each tiny grass and humble flower,
Each little fruit—or sweet or sour—
And bud and blossom on each tree,
Or fragrant leaf the eye can see,
All speak of God in thoughts sublime:
They see it traced in every line.
They see it written on each cloud,
Or hear it sound in thunder loud,
In tempest and in ocean's roar,
As dash the big waves on the shore.

They see it glow in stars of light,
Or twinkle in the dews of night,
In pebbles, and in grains of sand,
' On sea and sky, and flowery land;
Indeed, no spot that did not shine
Reflected from the hand Divine.

O happy, blessed, immortal pair!
What joy, what wealth of love they share.
But who would sing that rapturous song,
Sings not the Heaven-sent burden long.
Imparadised, God gave to man
The Law: the prohibition ran
Distinct; *The fruit of every tree*
Eat freely—and to thee and thine
Be joy—except which is most just,
Knowledge of Good and Ill thou must
Not eat or touch. Thus disobey
And thou therefor, that very day
Shalt surely die. They plucked, they ate—
Were driven from their fair estate!

One Sin,—and desolation wide
Sweeps on, an ever deep'ning tide—
Their every human power disarms!
Their spirits quake with wild alarms—
Are borne resistless to the doom
Of sorrow, labor and the tomb.
Time and Eternity! what cost!
They shudder—groan—with anguish tossed.
One sin,—her progeny, how dread!
Each, like Medusa's hydra nead,
From which a thousand eyeballs glare:
And woe and wrath are mingled, where
The forked tongue and barbed sting
Their venom-exhalations fling.

O miserable of happy days!
O dread reality! what praise
Is due to Him who wields the rod
Most just, of the avenging God!
Can He, the Holy One, above,
Restore to favor, trust and love?
Put off a space—and grant him time
In sorrow to repent his crime?

Man may find Grace ! Harp, lift thy
  voice !
Forever over Death rejoice !
Where is the Lamb? Harp, melt with praise !
God's Offering—"Ancient of Days."

O Prince of Heaven ! O Power of Grace
And matchless Beauty ! Leader, Chief,
Of that immortal host who trace
Thy glory in that grand relief
To mortals from their direful woes !
O Savior ! Prince ! whose heart o'erflows
With tenderness, Surprise of Heaven !
Imperial Delight ! whose brow
Stands thick with stars, whose life is given.
O Love unmeasured ! truly now,
Our Lord tents in the flesh; All Hail !
Uninterrupted joys unveil.
His mercy-guided arm supreme,
From ruin snatched our falling world
And bears aloft! O what a theme
For wonder, else it had been hurled
To utter wreck—now held in light

Of Heaven, well orbited its flight.
Hope in the bright'ning distance gleamed,
God Glorified, and man Redeemed.

CHAPTER IV.

TRIAL OF FAITH.

Where mountain precipices frown,
As gathering streams from raindrops down
Leap over jutting cliff and flow
Through winding gorges deep below—
Sweep fiercely on with gathering wrath
'Twixt spray-bedrabbled boughs their path,
Until a broadened river's bed
By hill and flowery valley led,
Reaches the sea.   'Twas thus the flood
Of surging wealth of birth and blood—
The eager motley crowd and vast—
The populace of every cast,
Thronging the Via Appia

And the Via Aurelia,
Down the Via Ardentina
And the Via Praënestina,
Appear—from streets suburban glide,
A full, resistless, restless tide.

Here met and mingled hoary age,
Poet, Philosopher and Sage,
The Commons and Pretorian Guards,
Women, to whom are given regards,
Who glide in fashions giddy whirl,
In tunic, turban, jet and pearl.
Each various group press on with will
Over the Capitoline hill,
Some down by the old Forum march
Before the temples and the arch
Of Titus; while wending along,
Ripples of wit and careless song
On many a lip, they hardly knew
Whither they went as forward through
Crowded streets of the city passed—
To reach through devious ways the sea
Rippling, of upturned faces full.

This wondrous confluent stream
Flows in—each face agleam—
Until a hundred thousand wait
Within the Coliseum gate.

Each side are terraced seats and long;
Around the vast arena throng
The multitudes. Within the wall
Wild savage beasts the heart appall,—
Huge lions from Numidias lands,
And wily tigers from the sands
Of Central Africa, and men
Dragged from the dark and dismal pen
Just opening. Behold, they come !
And suddenly the mighty hum
Of busy rustling lips is hushed,
The cheeks once colorless are flushed,
The eye is fixed, and silence reigns.
The prisoners, so late in chains,
Stand forth—beholding and beheld !
The walls completely sentinelled.

INSCRIPTIONS.

Deep in these crypts, Pastors of Rome
And worthies, found a quiet home.—Page 13.

Within this broad arena stand
A hundred Christians, hand to hand!
No marks of fear upon their brows,
Still unrecanted are their vows!
Roarings reverberate, for then
Fierce angry lions from the den
Leap wildly forth, casting a gaze,
Fixed, short and fiery, eyes ablaze—
On every side wild terrors shed.
With hungry gnawing maws unfed—
They paw, they roar, they gnash, they spring,
Till leaping far—they grasp, they cling
To each his victim—widely tear
The anguished body—laying bare
Fresh mortal wounds—drinking the flood,
The scarlet jettings of their blood.

One victim touched the heart, the home—
Dragged forth from subterranean Rome
To glut the tyrant Decius' rage—
Whose life with generous blessing frought,
His goodly name and hoary age,
And venerated service wrought,

Should shield—but nothing in these days
Can long divert the public gaze.
Unarmed, attended by the guards,
And standing forth a hundred yards
Or more, ere stretching on the bed
Of purple—making ready—said;
"O Emperor, I am, indeed,
A Christian! yet will not plead
My life. Know ye that I have fought
A goodlier fight than this—have sought
The joy, the love, the living peace
Within—Silver or gold allure
Me not—on Him the great surcease
Of sorrow, fix a steady eye.
In Christ I stand—nor aught can move
My purpose—what can I but die
For Him who wins me by his love
To Heaven." A mighty murmur rose—
Tumultuous storm by all his foes!
Thousands responsive cry—"Away
This superstitious sect this day!"
The old beheading block they brought
And battle-axe with figures wrought,

Thus doing, said: "The laws direct,
Thus always to this hated sect!"
That day who perished at his post
Was of Christ's sacramental host
A firm defender: truly well,
Like him on Pisgah's height, he fell
In sight of Heaven—of glorious prime—
Ripe for the golden harvest time.
His body, by permission, laid
Where loving earthly friends had made
Deep cemeteries in the walls
Of St. Callixtus. In these halls
Or chambers where they laid him, rest
Vast numbers of the unknown blest.

A day of carnage—many more
Within the wide enclosure thrust,
Defenceless maidens gently bore
Assaults—lo! fifty tigers rush
Bounding from dens on either side
And wildly round the centre glide.
O blood thirst Romans! such a heart
Of stone—what passion can impart

To pity? what mysterious fane
Receives such sacrifices slain,
Thirsts for the purple of this rite,
Drinks thus in this assembly's sight?
What cause? from the arena's sand,
Hark! hand in hand this fearless band
Raises a note of dying praise—
The echo of the coming days.

I.

How long, O Lord! holy and true,
Dost Thou delay avenging blood?
But Thine be done—thy purple flood
Can wash us white—our hearts renew.

II.

Thanks for the chastening of his rod,
To Him who raised our ruined race;
Who triumphed by Almighty grace,
And made us kings and priests to God.

III.

O Death, where is thy sting? O Grave,
God's subterranean road to bliss;

From such a dying world as this,
The Crucified—alone can save.

One by one their voices languish—
One by one with mortal anguish,
Are carrying on high their song—
Which they and all in Heaven prolong.
The struggle brief—the strong, the weak,
The beautiful, the sweetly meek,
The bold, the terrible, the wild,
Were mingled—hundreds there were piled,
Resolving in this furious fray.
The body to its mother clay—
The soul to Heaven—to each well done,
The envied martyr's crown is won
There was the hiding of his power—
The Christ in them—the glory hope—
There was the Christian's secret out
With victory their latest shout!
While thousands gazing, blindly grope
And weary of the passing hour.

Thus every way, they Christ proclaim.
The vast intent assembly see

The logic of their lives: they hear—
The "*unto Him who loved and washed*
Us in his blood;"—the ecstasy
Of hope—and thus, strong, deep and clear,
Witness the force of truth just flashed
Upon the mind or buried deep
Into the human will, to reap
The harvest which these deeds inspire.
As lingering multitudes retire,
The mingled words—" faith, hope and love,
Mysterious! their Christ above!"
Are heard distinct: from this sad day
Some in new accents learn to pray;
Some to the Catacombs retire;
Others at Christian homes inquire
The Way. Thus grew the living word,
Thus through the Capital was heard;
Patrician and Plebeian see,
Philosophers and bearded Priests,
The rulers of the sacred feasts
And Emperor and Guards agree,
That innocence and virtue shine
In man or maiden, young or old,

More than the golden wealth untold,
That overlays Apollo's shrine.

CHAPTER V.

PAGAN DEITIES.

Gods of the world—or far, or near—
And goddesses of love and fear!
Come quickly to these seven hights,
Mingle your various strange delights;
Where worshippers your statues rear—
Your Temple's sacred rights revere.
Come from Olympus, once again,
Father of gods and king of men;
With bright-eyed Juno, come once more—
Let Argus and her sons adore—
And all the fair ephemeral train
Of nymphs which boil the surging main.
Come from the ferry boat of Styx,
Come from the caverns of the Nyx,
Come from Hesperia shining far,

Come Sol and Luna's flaming car;
From where the golden apples grow,
And Aides' plunging rivers flow.
Come, dwellers on these lofty thrones
Where winter storms in howling tones
Triumphantly sweep ever on,
And ancient cedars bow anon;
Come where a grand libation's poured—
And gods and goddesses adored.

Goddess of Beauty! at whose shrine
Inferior deities resign
Their wonted loveliness and grace.
Whose brilliant countenances trace
From torrid clime to frigid cold,
From east unto the gate of gold,
No sweeter, softer, lovelit eyes—
Thy cheeks the rósy of the skies;
Lips gently parted, floating hair
Stirring the odor-ladened air;
Enchantress! now thy magic breathe—
Whose tender, warm and burnished glance
Quickens the step of sea-maid dance—

While Satyrs blooming garlands wreathe.
To thee, to thee, alone, is given
To hold serene the keys of Heaven,
Open the golden gated way,
And tip the Orient with day;
And Art and Grace extend thy fame
Through lands of every tribe and name.
From thee reflects a smile supreme.
For thee, the vine and wild flowers gleam,
The violet and asphodel
And hyacinth, odors expel,
In darkling bowers where wood-nymphs hide,
And silvery dancing waters glide.

Diana, goddess of the bow,
With lip and cheek and heart aglow!
Cease now thy chase and turn thee back
Over the hunter's mountain track—
Flashing, through forest glades so fleet
In shimmering shower or tropic heat—
Afar your ringing charming voice
Makes Nature's solitudes rejoice!

At thy approach, wild beasts retire.
Some in soft velveted attire
Of winter grey or summer robes
Betake to flight; with double globes
Gazing on thee in grove or sky,
Shrink at the notice of thine eye.
Come to this banqueting prepared,
Where Jupiter, the golden-haired,
Presides in high authority!

Come youthful Bacchus, quickly up
To banquet with the ruby cup;
Thy brewed enchantments throng the boards,
Each Bacchanal all joy affords!
Pleasure distills from brimming bowls
Where wealth and splendor gayly folds.
A retinue around thee throng
Of multitudes—in plight devout,
Elate, aglow, with feast and song,
With laugh and cheer and merry shout.
Hail Grape-dyed Visage, ever hail!
Thy presence hither must not fail:

Thy worshipers with cheek aglow—
What treasures to thy coffers flow!

And thou, swift Messenger to men
From gods of every grove and glen:
On beams of light with sunward eye,
Thy glinting white wings cleave the sky
New-fledged. Wing hither thy proud way,
Nor in the realms of beauty stray;
By streamlets of the mountain side,
Let crest of ebb or flowing tide
Hinder thee not,—thy message bear.
Apollo, with his golden hair,
Minerva's wit and wisdom bright,
Or Mars with bloody spear for fight,
Delay thee not; though Venus stays
To catch the lips of loving lays,
Or Juno sweeps her burnished car,
While Pan and Chaos reign afar!

Thou wind-winged Neptune!—full of glee,
Whose pinions swift as lightnings wild—
Lashing to storm-vexed waves the sea—

The briny deep of ocean piled;
Whose mighty voice with ceaseless roar
Curls like a wave along the shore.—
Thine is the happy ocean life—
A Mermaid for thy water-wife;
While Nymphs and Dolphins ever near,
Moved by their love, perhaps their fear,
Announce with voice of loud acclaim
The fame of thy far-sounding name!
Or each, on odor-ladened wing
Bears special honor to the king.
When hurried with thy whirlwind steeds—
Their limbs dipping the silvery spray,
Trampling the bed of soft sea weeds
Or rushing to the furious fray—
Champing their iron curb, they hurl
Thy chariot wheels with dashing whirl,
Careering as they wildly leap
The billows of the wrathful deep!

Ye gods and goddesses! so rife
With ancient wisdom, wit and mirth,
Flooding with chrismal light the earth—

Rock, grove and glen instinct with life!
Come ye, from where your presence breathes
From Nature's flowery lap where wreathes
The odored vine, the brimming fount
Sparkling—and from the sacred mount.
From Tempe's most romantic vale,
The verdant forest hights to scale;
From where Achilles' ponderous spear
Was wielded in his glad career;
Where giant Hercules once strove
To slay the beast of Nemea's grove.

Perhaps, upon thy hither way,
Some fairy hand may lead astray;
May tempt thy wandering feet awhile
To loiter, and the hours beguile;
Perhaps that Hermes with his lyre,
Prometheus with his sacred fire,
Or even Clio's tragic song
May tempt thee and thy stay prolong:
Should Dido still detain the night,
With sweet discourse thy heart delight;
Or Comus banquet at his board;

Or Plutos watch his shining hoard;
Should Ajax skim along thy path,
Or fierce Achilles swell with wrath:
Hold on thy way—nor stay thy flight
Till gods and goddesses unite—
A noble, mighty, surging throng,
In one convivial banquet song.

Come, where the high Athena leads!
Where stand the ready snorting steeds
Of Phœbus for his chariot race:
While toward Olympus' trembling base,
Minerva turns her piercing eye,
And lifts her radiant armor high!—
There quaffs the offerings paid again,
And visits the retreats of men—
To teach the grateful world her lore
Where mortal worshipers adore!
Ye grand celestials! well we know
That ages of the long ago,
Ye came to nerve the hero's arm,
To sound the trump of war's alarm,
Or fill the plains and hills with song;

To-day, rock, grove and glen prolong
The melody,—in wind and wave
Where the immortals breathe and lave,
Gay Nature's gladdest forms are rife
With spirit beauty and with life.

Rome's lofty hights that day were crowned:
That vast assemblage so renowned
Receiving each, libations poured
On altars reared to gods adored.
Their feastings under verdant groves,
Their songs and gayeties were passed;
Their curious and nightly loves—
And all the sweets of rich repast.
Thus served, one stood thereup:—his palm
Waved gently the profoundest calm—
And then a voice.—" Ye gods declare
To human kind, if now ye are
Apprized, *what earthly power can stay*
This superstition and this day
The ancient altar fires restore ?
The temple's service throng once more
With worshippers, whose sacred rites

Shall waft sweet incense from these hights?"
Then all that vast assembly, shout
Aloud ! *what logic like the sword*:
What argument unsheathed can rout
Our common enemy, afford
Relief like this ! *Far up the sky*
Reverberates the mingled cry
Of persecution; the air is filled
With scarlet words till hearts are chilled.

Then, first, began the evil days !
The saints of God pursue their ways
Diverging,—thus the people heard
The word of peace through Christ our Lord.
Some, to the rugged mountains fled,
Some, to the well worn paths blood red;
Others, to mighty cities came,
And some, alas ! to caverns deep—
The Catacombs of wondrous fame—
Came sadly to these tombs, to weep,
Perhaps to die; as while the days
Rolled on, crushing their earthly hope,
To linger where no sunlit rays

Illuminate the gloom—to grope
In darkness—*nothing but the light
Of the great God's eternal truth,*
Through all this labyrinthine night,
To light the heart of age or youth.

CHAPTER VI.

INCIDENTS.

As when the earth to summer wakes,
Or dawning of the morning breaks,
And Nature's radiant fingers trace
New beauties on her smiling face;
So Rome, the upper city, stands—
To issue to the world, commands:
The Rome, that Cæsars saw arise
Magnificent as Babylon,
Or Baalbeck, city of the Sun.
Luxuriant, beautiful and wise!
Stands where the generations toiled—
One, through a thousand fruitful years,

The haughty nations long despoiled
By war, to poverty and tears.

But what were arch, or dome, or tower,
To Rome embedded in the rock:
Or pomp of state, or regal power,
To those beyond the tyrant's shock!
Those still retreats—those quiet homes—
That glorious wealth of faith—that rest
That comes to saints—the ever blest
Asleep within the spacious tombs;
Martyrs, confessors,—virgins all,
Of Christ the True and Faithful One.
Beneath that canopy of wall
Their cross illumines like the sun
Our sky, scatters the dark—those rays
To light with sparkling gems their ways—
Soul scintillations all Divine,
Through many generations shine.

DEATH SCENE.

A SISTER, loving and beloved,
In radiant grace of womanhood

Adorned, as forth she stood—
Ere by the silent messenger removed,
Our equal in the rugged race
Of life. Youth's blush upon her face,
Her heart heaved like the throbbing sea
With generous impulse, and as free—
Then placid and reflecting back
The Heaven within. There was no lack
Of love, or tenderness, or joy.
With scarlet cheek and pallid brow,
We almost feared to ask her how
Her health appeared, as day by day
She faded from this world away:
As snowflakes on the river's brink,
One moment glistening ere they sink—
Or as some brilliant star of night,
Fades with the morning's dawning light—
So she as gently sank away,
As the last tints of closing day.

Long days and longer nights were passed
Before the longest and the last.
What memories still linger there—

The watchers' look, the tender care,
That midnight summons, and that bed
On which she suffering lay—the dread
Of such an overwhelming grief—
And God the only sure relief.
Tears from their deep'ning fountains leap
From eyes which unaccustomed weep,
Friends, relatives are gathered near—
Heart-treasures held in memory dear:
The Father bending, took her hand
In his—for Mother to the land
Of spirits long ago had passed
In peace—and pressed it close, then cast
A look of ardent sympathy:
The sisters, bowed with nightly care,
Brothers attending, too, were there;
Each, humbled now as hearts were riven
And wept, though not to weeping given.
Then with a voice distinct and clear,
No quivering of lip with fear,
She uttered that sublimest word
Of life and love—JESUS—then heard
That now the Messenger had come

Of death;—hushed be the whispered hum,
And mute the lip,—"I'm going now—"
While dewdrops gathered on her brow,
And silently the eye grew bright—
As then the spirit took its flight,
New-fledged for the immortal, far
Beyond the scenes that death can mar.

THE BLIND GIRL.

In Saint Cecilia's lowly crypt,
Where fossors in the tufa chipped—

There lived a gentle maiden fair,
With brow of light and curl of hair.—

At dawn, at evening, and at noon,
Queen of the fairest flowers in June;

With eye once tender as a child,
With cheek a crimson when she smiled.

But she was blind! the orbs of light,
Rolled in their ever-during night;

Her cheeks in awful darkness pale,
Fanned by no sweet refreshing gale—

Yet in her soul, a bright desire
Spangles the eye with kindling fire:

Through sombre avenues, her feet
Familiar press the winding street,

A guide, interpreter and friend!
Thus duty with devotions blend.

Confessors there with holy fear
Into this midnight darkness peer,

She grasped the hand of youth or age
Escaping from the Tyrant's rage,

And hurried on without delay
Along the dark and narrow way,

To holy shrines or chapels press,
Where Saints, all-joyful faith confess.

Rude graven thoughts, her fingers trace,
Of glowing deeds discourse with grace.—

THE FOSSOR.

"Diogenes, the Fossor, buried in peace on the eights before the calends of October."

There was the *anchor* rudely drawn,
Of hope so eloquent, the dawn.—

There the *true vine* her branches spread
Fragrant and fruitful overhead,—

The rustic flower in emblem new
Of Sharon's Rose—the Pure and True.

Here Divine Orpheus tunes his lyre,
And Argus *hundred eyes inspire.*

There the old Hebrew idyl glows
Where death-shade lingers to repose.

Her locks with drops of night are hung,
Love's ardent canticles are sung.

THE BURIAL.

How oft some burial service led
Saints to the City of the Dead;
Where no Italian sunshine glows,
Are many tears in anguish shed.

They lay a youthful form to rest,
Where no rude hands its sleep molest;

Brought hither by some loving friends,
Whose care their faithfulness attest.

The noble, bleeding corse is laid
In sombre avenue and shade;
'Mid crumblings of mortality,
The young, the beautiful must fade.

For he a valiant martyr, was
Obedient to the Roman laws;
Yet on the broad arena fell,
Victorious for the Master's cause.

Who gloried in the purple gore
As angry beasts his body tore,
Ambitious of a martyr's crown—
Reproach and shame, he meekly bore!

They crave his mangled form, to bear
Down to this quiet resting, where
So stealthily at midnight hour,
They lay with tears and pious care.

Hewed a new casket for him there—
Embalmed in aromatics rare—
So like the manner of his Lord.—
Clad in the white that angels wear.

Thus dearest friends—a noble throng—
Chanting the hymn and sacred song,
" My Soul return unto thy rest,"
Bear sorrowful, the corse along.

What they had known before, forsooth,
Saw through his narrow grave the truth,
A thousand times more light and clear,
That they had wept this fallen youth!

Death was, indeed, *his natal hour*—
The bud just opening to the flower—
The birthright of the soul above—
Now born a king, he reigns with power.

Sweet hope! the coming of that day,
When heaven and earth shall pass away;
The resurrection triumph won,
Sheds over each, her glorious ray!

One soul released from bondage here,
One soul retained in memory dear,
Till mortal to immortal wakes;
And joyful, Saints in Heaven appear.

PICTURES.

Sincere and honest doubter, pause—
Mark the *unfoldings* of this way;
At every step what wondrous scenes!
Look, that they lead thee not astray.

These Pozzolona grottoes speak—
Shall be the witness to thy heart;
Light through these marble tablets shine,
And life, joy, comfort still impart.

Lean heavy on the guiding arm,
To the Interpreter attend;
Your eye on every blazing line,
That ancient Hope and Faith defend.

Here classic pagan symbols blend—
Here Christian thought shines out anew—

The form, the drapery is old,
The spirit hid within is new.

Here figured is Diana's hart,
Drinking from flowing water brook—
The *soul* which hunted, thirsting, stands,
Quaffing with eager, anxious look.

The Cross, intensely loathed, abhorred,
The badge of infamy and shame;
Under the chrismal touch transformed
To glories that surround His name.

They see it in the fern and flower,
In bird that skims the rippling air,
The yard and mast of gallant ship,
In act of swimming and in prayer.

The Dove, that holy sign of faith,
Those light-winged coursers as they bear,
Not Venus' airy chariot,
But Grace, on gilded wheel rolls there!

No far-famed olive branch of peace
In great Minerva's woven crown,
But Christian—victor in the race
Which seemed to them of chief renown.

The hare, that burrows in the earth—
The lion, vigilant and bold—
The fiery steed whose course is run—
Types that some various truth unfold.

The Savior weary at the well—
From the five loaves are thousands fed—
His entry to Jerusalem—
The better wine when hearts are wed—

Here Daniel in the lion's den—
Three Hebrew children wrapped in flame—
Elijah's burnished chariot wheel—
And Jonah's grave of ancient fame—

The serpent and the lamb are there—
Here Israel's leader smites the rock—
Here Abraham's wondrous sacrifice—
Here the Good Shepherd leads his flock—

Thus carved on deep volcanic rocks,
Christ in a thousand forms is wrought—
Sacred to memory of Saints,
Which coming generations taught!

THE GOING FORTH.

As eagles on strong pinions rise,
Out of these caverns swiftly flies
The wondrous message of the skies.

Each spray-dash on Italian shore—
Each wave with curl and dash and roar—
Echoes the Gospel evermore.

Over the far-famed Apennine,
On lofty Alps—the Leapentine,
Or floats serenely down the Rhine.

From lip to lip the truths unfold—
From hill to vale new tidings rolled—
As the old Prophecy foretold!

Till Rome ablaze sent up her light—
To other cities in their might,
Chasing the darkness of their night.

Stroke followed stroke of wrathful foes—
The sun-burst scintillation glows
Till pilgrims bear unnumbered woes!

Men, women, children—hearts devout,
From sheltering homes are driven out,
Conflicts within, and fears without!

The story of the Cross, their song,
The tragedy of fearful wrong—
The wail of requiem prolong.

Through floods and flames the strangers sped,
Bearing the Bible as they fled—
Those sacred leaves in secret read.

The spirit's double-edged sword—
Cleaving the way to northern horde—
The idols of the people scored—

How their temples earthward tumble
And deserted altars crumble—
All the heathen gods to humble—

As they tell the wondrous story—
See the spreading of the glory
O'er the nations old and hoary!

The early dawn—the evening rays—
Full on the glorious Cross they raise,
Invites to tears of joy and praise.

Here seeds of every virtue trace—
Of wealth, of culture, every grace.
Begotten in this *lordly race.*

CHAPTER VII.

CLAUDIA.

There too—a daughter, lovely, fair,
With costly jewels,—talents rare—
Was Claudia just from the court
Of grand old Britain, where the king—
Her father, sought from many a port,
The rarest, costliest gifts to bring,
This royal princess to adorn.
The Orient her store unlocks,
Bright as the dew-gems of the morn,
The wealth of seas, the ore of rocks,
A charm to youthful beauty lent;
And from the frozen fur-clad north,
From wild Arabia's distant plains,
The heavy ladened camel trains
Bring aught that add to wealth or worth.
The shells from many distant isles,
The pearls from many a stormy sea,
And sweet gums from the tangled wilds,

Rare flowers adown the lonely lea,
Are hers,—the gift of father's care,
And mother's generous purpose share.
Here youth and beauty lend a charm
To all the fairest of the hour,—
The glitter of a jeweled arm,
And retinue of stately power;
And naught that pleasure can impart,
Or rounds of happiness secure—
Bewitching to the eye, the heart,
Where friendships ardently allure—
Could be denied the queenly maid;
For she the fairest of the fair,
No thought her gaieties invade—
Their liveliest entertainment there,
A token from each eye attests,
That she is queen of all the guests.

Then travel took her where she would—
To ruins grey, some stately pile—
City, and hill, and verdant wood,
Romantic spots of Albion's isle.
And on the Continent were traced

Far-famed resort and dreary waste;
The courts of European kings
Flung open to this fairy queen,
The changing spell of earthly sheen,
Where joy, though evanescent, springs.

Here first she heard Pretorian guards—
Who late had come from southern lands;
Who spoke of Christ, and his rewards,
And freely of his love,—commands—
That grace, that wondrous grace that bled,
And where the Spirit kindly led.
Indeed, the air was full of praise—
From ardent lips the tidings rolled;
The Peasant in his galley lays,—
And Kings with earthly crowns of gold,
Each worshipful his gift unites,
Which every heart to praise invites.

Far from her God she sits her down
In lonely solitude,—the crown
Of immortality abased—
Fruits blasted and her soul a waste:

Her former joyous hopes are fled,
Once buoyancy of spirits dead;
Once she could pray—but now the sky
Like brass echoes her Pagan cry;
Beneath, she treads the solid earth
With heart unmoved except by mirth,—
Soul,—like the plunging steel-clad bark
Still dashing on by day or dark;
What were the ballast to the ship?
Who holds the compass on life's trip?

Does Father yonder dwell—his Son
My Elder Brother? yet I shun
His awful, penetrating gaze,
While pressing hard Destruction's ways:
There, too, my Comforter and Friend—
My guides—a retinue attend;
But darkness gathers on apace,
And scale-dimmed eyes can hardly trace
The chart, that marks the rock and strand,
Or charter of the promised land.
Bewildered reason will not seek
To cling to God,—the arm is weak;

To walk there is a palsied limb,
The ear is heavy, eye is dim;
And feeble Conscience rocked to sleep,
Has tears, but not for me to weep.
O Wretchedness, unloose the chain
That binds me to a world of pain!
Each link that holds me from the Cross,
For earth seem as it may—*is dross!*
One grasp of soul the Word received,
Humbly and gladly, she believed;
As heartily obeyed that Word,
Just as the message read, she heard;
Plunged in Baptismal waters clear,
Put on new life deep hid in Christ;
Raised to new life that knows no fear—
That perfect love imparadised.
Henceforth the study of His word,
Whose, for her ransom, blood was spilt—
Her meat, her drink, for she had heard
Of hope on firm foundation built.
Her lips the choicest words distill,
That fell so sweet on mortal ear
Like honeyed nectar,—so his will
Scatters *aroma* far and near.

Nor could her ardent labors cease
Bearing the cross for Jesus' sake,
Till other hearts from sins release
Should to superior powers awake;
Till many souls had caught the flame
The spirit's kindlings began,
Living or dying for his name.
Supreme her love to God and man!
The Gospel triumphed in her hand!
For the poor peasant of the land
The fountains of her soul were moved—
Yearning in pity o'er the lost,
Well doing, blessing those she loved
At whatsoever earthly cost.

Her thoughts turned to her native isles—
Dear memories of childhood's land;
Where nature's glowing picture smiles,
Swaying young life with fairy hand;
She longs to breathe that air again—
Her feet to tread familiar ways—
The crowded mart, the quiet fane,
Where she had passed her youthful days;

'Bove all to speak the ancient word,
Which first, all-joyful, she had heard.

Thus noble Claudia,—thus on
The chalky cliffs of Albion,
The old—the tried old Gospel sped.
From vale to summit, and between,
The echo of her voice serene,
Fell in soft cadence, as she said:

I.

Seek ye the little wicket-gate!
To worldliness severely strait,
Which opens to the narrow way,
Leads on to everlasting day.

II.

Arching that gate, your eyes behold
In letters carved, embossed in gold;
These words, which calm each surging strife,—
"I AM THE WAY, THE TRUTH, THE LIFE."

III.

Now will you tread the heavenly way,
And learn to watch as well pray,

To wholly cast your sins away—
And Heaven's supreme commands obey!

IV.

Deny thyself, and enter in,
Unburdened of your load of sin;
Open your eyes upon the light,
And walk by faith, and not by sight.

V.

Let not the fear of mortal clay,
Nor Satan's wiles thy heart dismay;
With shield and sword and helmet strong,
The raging contest is not long.

VI.

Severely pressed, the foe will yield,
And Faith triumphant win the field;
In the Great Spirit's armor stand—
And triumph in the Glory-land.

VII.

Bearing aloft the prize as won,
Through Christ the everlasting Son;
Where the bright crown and palm await
Your coming at the pearly gate.

On every summer breeze there floats
The trumpet's warning clarion notes:
Brittania,—vale and mountain, heard;
Old Scocia's hights, the southern wave,
And dark ravines, that glorious word
Echoed again;—MIGHTY TO SAVE.

While Years advance with martial tread,
And each as swiftly onward sped;
Still Claudia longed to see the land
That Fancy touched with magic wand;
Land where the moonlight paints the glen
Rich with the glorious autumn hues;
Where with bright eye and keener ken,
The soul looks out on fairer views;
Where vines in rich profusion trail
And spices scent the teeming gale;
Where cities rise and costly spire,
And music swells from heart and lyre.
She longed to see the Fatherland—
Whence sprang of man that noble race
Who consecrate at God's command,
Life, happiness, time, honor, place.

" O, Italy, of thee, we sing!
" O, Rome, thou art our dream by night!
" To thee, our waking thoughts would
    cling
" To thee we turn, to catch thy light!"

She hither came. Nor yet could rest—
Ambitious to new ways explore;
Rich sacred temples were her quest,
Lips touched with hallowed fire the more:
She dwelt not on the buried past,
On martial Rome's imperial head;
On battle fields, o'er cities vast,
Or where long-honored heroes bled;
Where brave and gentle Brutus fell,
Livy and Tacitus excel;
Where Virgil's honored mother wept,
And Horace' festal hours are kept;
Her piles of marble, dome and tower—
Symbols of luxury—empower.

She lingered not where lofty walls
Garnished with vast and precious stones,

Or grandeur of her public halls,
Display the power that wealth enthrones;
Nor where 'mid Pagan rites and prayers
A thousand altars flaming on,
Their devotees allegiance swear
Under the dome of Pantheon:
Nor lingered she in pendant shade
Where deities profane invade,
Where incense far perfumes the gale,
And goddesses at feasts regale.

But Claudia sought, and not in vain
The home of many a faithful one—
She heard the story of the slain,
How their blest earthly life had flown;
She read the story of their wrongs
On the brief records of the past,
Their tragic death, their latest songs,
And the bright nimbus overcast.
They looked beyond the narrow bound
That horizoned their earthly way,
The kingdom they had fully found,
The coming of the perfect day:—

THE SECRET STAIRS.

Then hand in hand securely locked,
Down through the caverns deep and lone,
Descending slowly on the stair
Each step advancing—place with care.—Page 87.

And O, what transport filled her breast
To seize at once the martyrs' crown—
Whose lives and glorious deeds attest
What they esteemed of chief renown!

She threads adown the Appian Way
Under the slant of sunshine ray,
Where Nature's lavish hand is flung,
And Titus' royal arch is hung;
Or where that mossy crumbling pile
Marks well the graves in narrow file:
Enters a garden wall enclosed
In hush of beauty all reposed,
Except a footfall,—turning round
She sees a friend, a guide is found;
Then hand in hand securely locked,
Down through the caverns deep and lone,
Descending slowly on the stair
Each step advancing—place with care:
The way is often angled, blocked,
And thick with many dangers strewn.
When suddenly a gleaming light
Fills her with gladness and surprise;

Before the unaccustomed sight,
A wondrous congregation rise,—
There in that darkened hush and hour
A temple service, filled with power.

She came—she saw—she heard anew
Of Christ the ever Pure and True;
Such love, such melody of praise,
Soul service wrought in works and ways—
Their prayers, thanksgivings, all inspire;
Each heart ablaze with new desire!
There where a thousand symbols shine—
Inscribed upon emblazoned walls,
Their faith, ennobling every line,
Lighting the corridors and halls,
So struck her eye while onward led—
Bowing upon the pavement cold,
With spirit deeply moved, she said;—
Behold, the half was never told!
O happy service! happy they
Who stand in presence of the court—
Who stand to catch the gracious word!
Blest be the Lord that taught the way!

It was indeed a true report,
Exceeding all the fame we heard!

What galaxy of wondrous charms!
Calming the soul to love's repose,
Where persecution's dire alarms
Spread terror to increase their woes.
The drooping spirit soothed to rest,
Or plumed anew on wings of power,
Sweet *meditations* fill her breast—
Faith's welcome solace for the hour.

"To Him of Calvary, God gave
"All power in Heaven and earth:
"He now is able souls to save,
"Save to the uttermost, his own,
"To keep against that day so fair
"What is committed to his care—
"Able to do exceeding more
"Than all we ask or even think—
"Succor the tempted from his store,
"And vast inheritance to link
"With those who sought and found—

"Able to make all grace abound—
"Able to keep us by his grace,
"And purify from base alloy;
"Present, before his Father's face,
"Whose presence is exceeding joy.

Here—life is short, uncertain, frail,
There—stores exhaustless, never fail.

Here—Satan, Sin and Darkness reign;
There—Heaven with all his glorious train.

Here—love of self—what base alloy!
There—love that heightens every joy.

Here—cares and wants perplex the mind,
There—calmed, a full fruition find.

Here—our faint hearts would seek some friend,
There—friendship pure and true—no end.

Here—Faith is fettered, bound by sense,
There—knowledge, pure, sublime, intense.

Here—garments grimed or stained in fight,
There—robed in everlasting light.

Here—in these narrow halls we wait,
There—enter at the golden gate.

Here—*in these caverns fain would rest,*
There—in the mansions of the blest.

Here—clouds so oft by storms are rent,
There—mirror-skies are o'er us bent.

Here—our best works our souls alarm,
There—perfect love our fears disarm.

Here—our best thoughts defiled by sin
There—joys without, and peace within.

Here—faith and hope our only sight,
There—both are lost in Heaven's own light.

Here—oft o'er others' woes repine,
There—every joy of Saints be mine.

Here—time though brief our souls employ,
There—everlasting is the joy.

Time, on her ever-changing tides,
Bears every child of earth along;
Thus she upon life's billow glides,
Catching the notes of spray-dash song,
Which o'er her form from day to day
Fling silvery drops among the grey:
But Mercy's bow was o'er her bent,
When lo! at last the lip was dumb—
For now on shining wing had come
The Angel of the Covenant;
And she was ready to depart
With him to the supernal field,
To drop the mortal, earthly part—
To Heaven her spirit calmly yield.

In Saint Cecilia's noble crypt,
They laid her body down to rest;
In the new niche the fossors chipped,
Where no rude hands the form molest.
With marble slab that niche they close;

Inscribing there,—*She Sleeps in Peace.*
The *nimbus* and the *crown* inclose—
The *urn* bespeaks the soul's release—
That *monogram,* of Christ the True,
And Cross, *deep-stained with rosy hue.*

CHAPTER VIII.

ROME.

Lo! this is Rome, Imperial!
The City of the Seven Hills!
Where Cæsars sat—the Capital
From which went forth the power that thrills
The world—whose growth a thousand years
Precedes a thousand of decline!
Wrapped in their vision, holy seers
Beheld thy sway upon the earth,
Who on the *scarlet beast* rode forth;
Round whom the nations' flags unfurled,
That saw thee Mistress of the World!

Afar the reed-roofed cabins gleam
Beside the Tiber's classic stream—
A lowly village year by year
Expanding in its various sphere
Grew on in wealth of pride and state!
At sunrise—and the gleaming gate
That walled it in was open flung,
As the world's long majestic train
Of commerce entered, and there hung
The drapery of her golden gain.
Labors immense! the nations bring
Their gifts of gold and pearls, and fling
Them at thy feet—they bring the wines
And myrrh and balm to glowing shrines,
Enriched with costly spoils of war—
Till name and fame are heard afar.

Grandeur on grandeur rises here!
All things that strike the eye, the ear,
With eloquence; the far-famed Arts
From Egypt and the classic fields
Of Greece! Each grove and temple yields
Inspiring thought, delight imparts:

THE CITY OF ROME.

O, Rome, thou art our dream by night!
To thee, our waking thoughts would cling—
To thee we turn, to catch thy light!—Page 85.

The beautiful, the wondrous here,
Where *Horace built his monument
More durable than brass;* and here
Sweet Virgil to the Muses lent
His genius in *a tale of woes.*
That stream of human life that flows
Impetuous, turbulent, and wide,
On to the Forum—long the pride
And center of their universe—
Bespeaks illustrious praise to Rome:
Out from whose arch or shaded dome
The joyous multitudes disperse,
Or in the Senate Chamber meet
The mighty spirits of this free
Republic; and we ne'er forget
That mandates, eagle-winged, went forth
To vex or bless a troubled sea—
And every corner of the earth!

Lo! this supremest power of Rome,
Pagan or Papal, both are one
In spirit and in work the same!
Highest on the Imperial throne—

Great Persecutor—arm of power—
Wielding her sceptre over kings
And priests—stands ready to devour
The church of Jesus Christ, or flings
Anathemas upon the Saints!
Each demon crime without restraints
Is bought and sold; beneath the sun,
Never more fearful deeds were done:
Pretending for each direful ill,
The sanction of the Holy Will!
How fallen! in that fall so low,
She takes and keeps the highest seat—
Sits musing o'er her pomp and woe—
Wealth, honor, crouching at her feet.

O land of Moloch and of blood!
Land of the rack and chain and fire;
Whose martyrs swell the purple flood
From prison walls and dungeons dire;
Insatiate One! what numbers more
Of human victims aud their gore,
May yet appease thy wrath, the while
Thy thousand incense altars smoke,

Ten thousand masses blood invoke;
While heretics the earth defile,
Whose garnished priests thy will attend;
Penance and gaudy pomp there blend
In worship at thy fragrant shrine;
Thy suppliants every power resign!
What festivals of public thanks
Are given, and the uplifting ranks
Of men in slow and solemn praise!
Their gifts they wave, they lowly bow,
They pay each consecrated vow,
In temples rich in costliest gift
Of Orient kings, which radiant lift
Their arches over relics old—
The images of saints, the mold
And bones in urns of pious dead,
Where ancient martyrs holy, bled.

O Rome, *thou Mother of all War!*
What time Omnipotence that speaks
The word, shall call thee to the bar
Of Justice, what ye proudly seek—
He gives to thee in rich reward;

Double far all thy sins abhorred !
Worthy—when God shall hold the cup
Of woes and bid thee drink it up;
Worthy—for thou hast drank the blood
Of Saints and Prophets martyred long—
And now He pours that scarlet flood
Into thy cup, for he is strong
Who renders judgment 'gainst the wrong.

But lo! the martyr's cry goes up—
How long O Lord, holy and true,
Dost thou withhold the mingled cup
Of gold—within of lurid hue,
Which brings remembrance to Him
Of all their woes, their groans and tears,
The rising incense of their hymn
Of praise, the quiet of their fears !
O Latinos, whose empire fills
The land, who sits on seven hills
In deeply scarleted array,
Who rules with most despotic sway
Where Oriental monarchs bow,
And in supreme allegiance vow,

Eternal faith—and to thy foes
Should one thy stately steps oppose,
Eternal enmity—or pour
The vials of thy vengeful ire
Of seething pitch and waxen fire,
On those who only Christ adore!

For now, the rest a little while
Is past; the number of the name
Is read—the Saints in long exile
Have numbered the prophetic days;
The wicked stand, enwrapped, amaze,
The seven angels all aflame
Have poured the vials of their wrath;
The time and times and half a time
Are now fulfilled complete, and earth
Receives the wages of her crime:
That day so long foretold, begins—
Rolling her thunderings ireful,
And Babylon is brought to full
Remembrance for her covert sins!

Meantime a flaming angel stood
On high, and cried with mighty voice;—

"Associate now the brotherhood,
"Receive the fullness of your choice;
"Priest, Prince and Potentate, and men
"Of war assembled—be dispersed!
"Blind be the eyes of keenest ken,
"The strongest arm be palsied then,
"As from Jehovah's lips accursed,
"Bow, arrows, ready at command—
"Are smitten from thy trembling hand!
"Your armor furbished from the rust,
"Now gird it—and be dashed to dust!"
And lo! at once on Zion's hights,
Ten thousand of the Saints there stood
Fortressed—with them like flaming lights
Angels encamp, as if they would
Behold the awful wondrous scene,
Calm as the morning, and serene;
And with them stood the Lord, faithful
And true, the ever Wonderful,
The written, yet the unknown Name;
Clad in a vesture dipped in blood,
With many crowns upon his head,
Whose eyes are as a burning flame,

Whose name is called the "Word of God!"
He the victorious armies led,
And to the thunders sound and light
A-flash of Heaven, in glistening white
They lead anew the battle on.
The nations tremble from afar,
Sin drives them on to ruin, death,
Each citadel and garrison—
Consumed by the Almighty's breath—
Then fall, confounded, in the dust.
Tyrants, Prince, Priest and Potentate,
The Scarlet Beast and lying Seer,
Dominions fall, and thrones—with lust
Of kingly power and pomp of state!

For seven days the battle slew—
The sword devoured—the spear, too, drank
The gushing streams of scarlet hue
Of Prince and Peasant, every rank;
And to this sacrificial feast,
Spread in Hamonah's darksome vale—
Where fell the horse, and horseman pale—
Each feathered fowl invited came;

With them the prowling woodland beast,
To eat the flesh of rank and fame!

And lo! another angel stood
And cried aloud;—" Fallen! fallen!
"Is Rome! is Rome! old Babylon!!
" The Queen in weeds of widowhood!—
" Plague, famine, pestilence and war,
" And mourning in the selfsame day!
" Alas! that all the world abhor
" Thee now—so proud, so weak, so gay!
" Alas! alas! that Babylon
" The great—should fall to rise no more!
" Merchants of gold and silver store,
" Stand afar off and cry anon;—
" Alas! alas! that no man buys
" The rarest of her merchandise—
" Her odors, ointments, wine and oil,
" Her precious stones each wrought with toil,
" Fine linen, purple and sweet woods;
" Her iron, ivory, marble, brass,
" Her silks and scarlet-tinted goods,

"And all the stores that wealth amass;
"Fine flour and wheat, and beasts and sheep,
"Horses and chariots, and slaves!
"And traders in the souls of men,
"Now gnash their teeth — they mourn — they weep—
"Standing afar by open graves,
"Or hidden in some dismal den!"

I.

Where are thy gods, O Rome, and where
The pallid chargers of the sea,
Which toss aback their foam-white hair—
Moulder forgotten on the lea,
Or in dim-lighted coral caves
Beneath the ever-shifting waves?

II.

Where are thy mist-robed sea-maids fair,
Those fishy monsters, filmy-eyed,
Who nursed their young with tender care,
Or taught them through the wave to glide;
To whirl, or dash, or dance, or leap,
With the veiled darklings of the deep?

III.

Queen of the cities of the earth!
Magnificence adorns these hills.
Thy luxury and wine and mirth,
Rich with the spoil thy coffers fills;
While tower and minaret so proud
Seem but to part the floating cloud.

IV.

Almighty God! Thy power alone
Will break the altars wreathed with gold;
Temple and idol, carved in stone,
Shall crumble back to dust of old;
And rites, with priestly pomp and grand,
Stay not the ruin of thy hand.

V.

The Cross, the conquering sign of Heaven,
Triumphantly the battle leads—
No more to Catacombs are driven,
The Martyrs of these bloody deeds;
The distant dawning is begun,
Love's victory will soon be won!

VI.

No more—great Triton blows his horn;
No veiled Minerva arbored there;
No more Wave-Neptunes rage in scorn—
Or Mercury's dread message bear;
The ancient temples, altars, fire,
Forgotten as Apollo's lyre.

Rejoice! your hallelujahs sing;
Forever over her rejoice
Ye Prophets and Apostles! bring
Your praise ye holy men! rejoice
Ye blessed Saints of memory dear—
Ye Servants, moved with holy fear!
Praise ye the Lord, the small, the great,
And thousands that before him wait:
Sing loud! Salvation now is come—
And glory, honor, power and might—
Old enemies in silence dumb—
The Lord our God has judged the right!
As ocean wave with spray bedewed—
With sound of mighty thunderings,
Responsive to earth's multitude

A voice answers, "Amen." Heaven sings
The echo to his praise,—"Amen."
Forever, evermore. *Amen.*

CHAPTER IX.

COMING OF CHRIST.

Sweet as the notes of warbling song—
Too swiftly have the years swept by;
Which memory remembers long—
But Happiness counts not the hours:
As when the speedy traveler's eye
Takes in the landscape—mountain towers
Or fruitful plains retiring back—
Its dim and shadowy outline left,
So we upon the winding track
Of years are gone—viewing each cleft
Of thought uplifted by our God,
From morn of life till dewy eve:
But ardent memories lingering grieve
Not of the persecutor's rod—

Transmuted to the finest gold—
The dross of earth, to wealth untold.

Bright was the morning, when the gray
Of twilight heralded the Day—
That day fixed for our Lord's return,
So long foretold by Prophet-bard—
Who scarce his coming could discern.
As when at the primeval word,
The sun first visited our world—
In daily duty unremiss—
Some fragrant leaf or op'ning flower
At every balmy breath unfurled;
So, now in splendor rose to kiss
Away with light the darkest hour.

That edge of morn with wonders full,
With mingled hues, how beautiful!
Skirtings of purple, blue and gold,
Girt the horizon and enfold!
The cloud-built temples of that morn,
With spire and minaret and dome,

Reflected far, the earth adorn;
And night-gems from the leaflets hung,
Fade, as Æolian zephyrs roam
Her courts and corridors among.

The earth from stilly night reposed,
In Nature's glad attire awaits;
Renewed with cloud and light enclosed,
As if to pass the opal gates:
When lo! a radiance fills the sky—
Th'Archangel's trump afar is heard!
The Sons of God at once draw nigh
And shout to their descending Lord!
The stillness of that moment breaks—
Of resurrection—which awakes
The long deep slumbers of the dead.
Saints of the Catacombs now break
Their sweet repose, in triumph led.
Behold, in twinkling of an eye,
The living sons of God are changed—
Resplendent like the saints on high—
Their robes of sordid dust exchanged,
Are with them wafted on to life

Eternal—now beyond the strife
Of earth, encamping on the cloud
With Heaven's beatitudes endowed.
With Him of Cavalry, they wait
The preparations to renew
The war on earth, or celebrate
The glorious gifts to tried and true,
Of approbation—and assign
Each station and reward Divine.

Meantime the vast, the wordly mass
Of vain profession! Where—alas,
Were they the unrepentant? left
Without excuse, without a hope;
Left as they lived—their way to grope
In utter gloom—to seek the cleft
That hideth from the wrath of God;
Whose judgments like a shiv'ring rod
Fall on their works. This evil day
Of wrath on all the nations came—
Not yet, indeed, the final day
Of retribution and of shame,
That gives to each of human race

His due reward—but yet a time
The earth had never seen before
Of violence of riot—more
Of war and pestilence and crime,
And more of murder and revenge,
Keen avarice and miry lust:
Earth's noblest faculties in dust—
One sin doth other sins avenge.

The angry nations rise and dash
With threatening aspect boldly on—
Against their war-reefs fall a crash
A shiv'ring wreck, world wide upon
The rocks, where others in their turn
Are hurried on—and scarce discern
The judgment omens of that hour
Of Unseen Hands' uplifted power!
Ah wretched world! What fires of hell!
Were never tongue or passion fed!
With angry thoughts proud bosoms swell—
To every social virtue dead!
Dead—though the eye with beauty shines,
Sweet melodies the ear delight,

The heart some golden form enshrines—
Love Heavenward never plumes its flight!
How strange—that the eleventh hour
Should find them unrepentant still,
Who often trembled at His power,
Yet yielded not the stubborn will.
This was the brief reply, God gave
A clamoring, unbelieving world;—
Afar the flag of hope unfurled—
"*The Gospel is the power to save.*"
So plain, so perfectly distinct,
The feeblest mind fails not to trace
The wealth of love with which is linked
The highest good of human race.

Hither, the Master's stay is brief.
Behold Him coming in the cloud!
He comes for judgment and relief,
A million legions strong, endowed
With power! a million Martyrs there,—
Who rose upon the flames with prayer,—
Beheaded on the witness block,—
Or slain from caverns of the rock!

No mark of beast upon the brow,
No image-worship sealed their vow;
They live on earth—with Christ they reign!
Who with the key of Satan's chain,
Comes in the kingdom of the Blest!
Once haughty nations own his sway,
The tongue of enemies is dumb,
Long typified by Sabbath day—
Earth's glorious jubilee is come!
The year septenial of rest—
One seventh, and the last and best!
The world is hushed, is calm, reposed,
In faith, in hope, in love and grace;
Old enemies made friends embrace,
And Janus' temple gates are closed!

The world is changed to glorious praise.
Nature puts on her robes anew.
The valleys decked for autumn days,
The fruitful hills in purple hue.
The fragrant morning's dawning light
Sheds on the forests as they rise,
From out the darkness of the night,

The wonders of a glad surprise.
From every gilded globe of dew
That sparkles on the leaflet gay,
There rises incense pure and new
To Him of everlasting day!
On gently sloping rays of light
The raindrops as they fall, ascend;
And in the gladness of their hight,
The melody of praises blend.
While every tuneful shrub and tree,
Or brooklet under snow or shade,
Now fill the air with music free,
Rejoicing that they thus were made:
Some gold-fringed violets look up
And fill their tiny velvet cup;
Roses rejoicing drink the dew,
And leaf and flower their tints renew;
Half blossomed and half hid with fear,
Kindly on them a heavenly tear
In all its gentle softness steals,
'Till every youthful flow'ret feels
Constrained to blush, when morning light
Has scattered all the shades of night:

Enough, if grateful tributes rise
Now—ever fragrant to the skies.

With what Divine, what unseen hand,
What latent force at his command,
In nature's laboratory wrought—
New Heavens and Earth—the brightest thought
Of ages spans with hope the tomb,
Arching the subterranean gloom.
Breaks on the world this Sabbath Morn,
The field, the hill, the vale newborn!
What silent forces at his call
Unlock their stores! the waterfall,
The bud just bursting into life,
Zephyrs with sweetest fragrance rife;
Life forces to each atom cling,
Life currents through the pulses spring;
Each ripened fruit, or sweet or sour,
Or medicated leaf or flower;
Beauty, utility and grace,
Here meet and mingle and embrace!

Yet better still—the heart of man
A nobler sacrifice can raise;
Unfolding God's all wondrous plan,
Transmuting every power to praise:
The intellectual grasp above,
The quick emotions waked to love,
And both to human will subdued—
And each to God; whose power renewed,
Whose thought and feeling and whose will,
Sublime capacities can fill.
Fair pluming faith and downy hope,
To cherub Charity the wings;
Piercing beyond the earthly cope,
New happiness to being brings;
The Spirits' ripened fruitage falls—
Joy, gentleness, and peace and grace,
Zeal upward, onward, loudly calls—
To win the prize—to gain the race!
True knowledge of the Word Divine,
That rends the veil of flesh away;
Exalting Christ in every line,
Lets in the pure and perfect Day.
The *eye* with living fire is lit,

The *ear* to Heavenly music thrills,
Whose parted *lips* the truth emits,
Whose answering prayer his word fulfills;
His *feet* on loving errands press,
His ready *hands* supply our needs;
Such living sacrifice is blest—
Man set apart to holy deeds.

Where once the clang of war was heard
Honors to victors are conferred.
Where sword and spear in battle raged,
The hand with glittering hand engaged,
With passion fierce and terror wild
The rider and the horse were piled,
Where flash and fire marked out the way
Of death and ruin and dismay,

The cloud is lifted—there the Light
Chases the dark of Error's night;
The Sun of Righteousness a-dawn,
In lavish beauty tints the lawn;
And the wide world with rapture glows
That War is changed to Love's repose.
That glorious Day *uplifts the Cross,*

So long obscured by wrath of foes,
Free from admixtures of earth's dross—
Once more illuminated—glows!

And the set time so long foretold—
To favor Zion as of old,
Is fully come—and David's throne
And Prince of David's royal line
To Israel is at once made known!
His virtues and his glories shine,
And Judah's land long desolate,
Reverts again to old estate.
Old Lebanus with hoary locks
Lifts up her cedared mountains spurred,
Sharon is made a fold of flocks,
The vale of Achor, for the herd;
On Jezreel's broad and fertile plain,
Prosperity and Beauty reign;
The land with milk and honey flows,
Afar, luxuriant verdure glows;
The lonely wilderness and place
Of solitude for them are glad;
The desert wears the blooms of grace,

Which ever grateful fragrance add;
Tabor and grand old Hermon rise,
Like sentinels, the dawn salute;
Each Wave from Gallilee replies,
Bashan and Carmel shake their fruit.

Whose Light is come! arise, and shine!
Ye sons of Jacob's royal line!
While Gentiles catch the rising Light
That shines away the darkest night!
And who are these that fly as clouds,
Or as the doves in eager crowds,
From continents and isles at sea
Sound forth their wondrous Jubilee?
Are borne along by Gentile kings?
Each nursing queen her offering brings,
To Him who reigns on Zion s hight
In glorious majesty and might.

The Lord, Himself, shall welcome them
His Servants to Jerusalem!
Within a fruitful land and fair
Whose name is given?--THE LORD IS THERE,

Whose walls are in these latter days
Salvation, and whose gates are Praise!
His shoulders bear the golden key
That opens earth to liberty;
Then shall be heard his glorious voice
With angry lightnings of his power,
The friends of Israel rejoice—
Her enemies the flames devour!
Mountains and vales from sin refined,
God calls for blessings on the soil;
His ancient promise brought to mind—
Plenty of corn and wine and oil—
A goodly land of brooks and vales,
Hillsides are fanned with fragrant gales;
The tresses of the tangled vine,
The wheat, the fig, the choicest wine,
The grazing herds, the flocks at hand,
The well filled dwellings of the land—
In which there is no lack of bread,
Though the vast multitudes are fed.

O wonderful of wondrous days!
Earth filled with hallelujahs, praise!

How fair the Prince's daughter, then,
Of Zion's hill, a citizen
Of no mean city; fair to view
As Lebanus, and pure and true;
Clad in her robes immaculate,
To rest a little while, to wait
The glory that shall follow when
The sons of Heaven with keener ken,
Behold the changes wrought by Grace,
And Providence for human race.
In Zion reigns eternally,
The Lord—that Sun of Heaven ablaze;
Before his ancients gloriously—
The Wonderful—the Prince of Days.

CHAPTER X.

FINAL TRIUMPH.

Eternal Love! to whom is due
The highest praises, pure and true.
Thou, whom the far Creation sung
While yet the morning stars were young;
Whom Shepherds on the tuneful reed
Or Prophets, taught the Chosen Seed;
To whom was smote the Hebrew lyre,
Or kindled fragrant incense-fire.
Where e'er thy dwelling place may be—
That mount that watched the forked sea
Where deep-toned thunder and the flame
Proclaimed in majesty thy name,
Or yet in Sharon's quiet vale
Rose-scented by the evening gale,
Or in the bush—dwell Thou with me;
Thy presence guide my thoughts to Thee,
God of my fathers, and my God!
Jehovah: holy, just and good;

Shiv'ring the nations with thy rod,
Yet moved to tenderness that would
Have gathered all into thy fold !
Redeemer ! what a wealth untold,
Unsearchable—great God—in Thee !

But say—thou messenger of good,
Thou that in Shushan's palace stood—
Who touched, greatly beloved, the man,
As evening sacrifice began;
Say *first, in what ill-fated flood,*
Has One his garments dipped in blood ?
Whose guests, and from what Heavenly hight
Are come arrayed in spotless white ?
Why dainties served, and wine is poured
To those around the royal board ?

Perhaps, thou oft hast heard of Him
Of Calvary, with bruised limb
And aching heart, the Morning Star
Of God's Eternal Throne; *afar*
His rays shot through the darkness dense;
Man glorified in Him, and hence

Their right to all the courts of Heaven—
Thus freely vast delights are given,
Of ornament and splendor; far
As eye can trace these glories are!
This is the wondrous marriage feast—
The supper of the Lamb! The least
Of all the Saints in glory crowned
Where new and pure delights abound,
Ascribe unceasingly their praise
To Him who first in other days
Reclined with them a spousal guest;
And whose beloved on his breast
Partaking, was supremely blest.

Hither, the high Celestials throng—
These Dominations, Princedoms, Powers,
That swell the everlasting song
Around the New Jerusalem towers;
They from embattlements there view
Those who an eager wing pursue
Their high dispatch—to worlds fulfill
The Sov'reign purpose of his will:
As once on dashing wheels of flame

For grand Elijah charioteered,
The sapphire coursers onward came
And the Celestial City neared:
Or when a pilgrim from the vale
Of poverty and tears, and pale
With human fears and earthly woes,
Just from the conquest of his foes,
Him, hither with observant eye
Beheld upborne, cleaving the sky—
With one white-winged on either hand
Sweep over vales of flowery land,
Or over lofty mountain hights
Which stand like sentinels in sight
Of Paradise, pursue their way
Sublime—no thought or wish to stray.

O joy! that these with beauty rife,
From that perennial Tree of Life
Should pluck first fruits, from Zion's Fount
That springs fast by the sacred mount
Drink draughts of everlasting joy—
While grateful songs their lips employ.

O what a glorious multitude,
No man could number, never viewed
Before by mortal eye—now pure—
Now sanctified in Him—secure
The right of king and priestly rank—
Who from His cup of sorrows drank—
For these were pilgrims who afar
Caught light from Bethlehem's beaming Star,
Who saw that rising, rolling flame
Which from "Destruction's City" came.

That day, ye well remember, when
The shining world once built for men
Reposed in silence; and the hour
The fiat of Almighty power
Went forth, and all the host of Heaven
There stood beholding, and were given
To view the conflagration: till—
O what a change had passed—his will
The ancient Prophecies fulfill!
Great day of fire from Heaven—the day
Of terrors and of dread dismay—

And wrath on all the human race!
To the impenitent despair—
That evil hour within the snare
Were taken, which their hands had laid.
Not so the righteous, these arrayed
In robes of uncreated light,
By Him whose hand of Heavenly might
Held fast the seven stars and chain,
And keys of Pluto's gloomy reign.
A wondrous day—the world in flame
When blessed Saints rejoicing came—
Prophets, Apostles, holy men,
*The Martyrs of the Ages, then
Rejoiced;* the day foretold so long
Had come: the universal song
Of hallelujah rose on high,
When as a mantle all the sky
Was wrapped in many a curtain fold,
And the broad gleaming clouds were rolled
Like parchment, and the earth so fair,
So lovely, so adorned with care,
Woodland and lake, and rolling sea,
Each storm-dashed rock and tuneful tree,

Her sun-bright robes, her gay attire,
Behold how changed—*dissolved by fire!*
Then, with a splendor unsurpassed
Lit up; magnificent and vast—
Earth shone afar—but not as now
In magnitude the first. *Lo! how*
Supremely wonderful and grand,
The world refashioned by his hand!
A glorious Church—snatched from the wide
Wide ruins—now a blushing bride—
And to this joyous banquet led
By Zion's grand *Imperial Head!*

Why stand amazed, my friend ? this day
Of Love triumphant, shall repay
Ten thousand times the dreadful cost,
Though worlds aflame—dissolve—are lost.
What power could snatch from these dire
    woes,
But Thine; O mighty Prince ! thy foes
Are vanquished! Sing ye Saints aloud'
And ye Redeemed! *let a sweet cloud*
Of incense rise, O ever rise

The arched rotunda of the skies—
To fill with Heaven's sublimest praise,
Caught up, prolonged by angel lays.

A Virgin, lo! Imperial born!
Bedecked with tints of rosy morn.
One hand the harp of glory bears,
And one the palm of triumph wears;
Flashes, the finger's burnished gem,
And brow with radiant diadem;
Each waving lock ambrosia breathes,
A myrtle vine of beauty wreathes;
Neck-chains of molten jewels hung—
Around her form the purple flung;
The rainbow hues of many a fold
Flashes large clasps of beaten gold;
A zone encircling her waist,
Her robes the flaming girdle graced;
Then over all, a veil of white,
Begemmed with shimmerings of the night;
As forth with gliding step she moves—
While Heaven with shouts of joy approves.

What time Messiah's praise we sing!
Grace, fairer than the sons of men
Is poured upon his lips; girding
His sword upon his thigh, shall then
With all prosperity ride forth—
Because of righteousness and truth.
Illustrious Son! the heir alone
Apparent to the Father's throne,
Whose sceptre is forever right—
Therefore thy God anointed him
With oil of gladness and perfume
Of Myrrh, in palaces of light
Above—more than his fellows, Him
We now adore, his praise resume
Who sought and brought with love and pride
From yonder world this ransomed bride
To the Paternal mansion; where
His servants as are wont, prepare,
Flashing from love-exchanging eyes,
His welcome, and this glad surprise.

O what a patrimony this!
That these His glory may behold,
Sit down with worthies, know the bliss
Which to their wondering minds unfold
As they behold Him face to face.—
The Great Omnipotent, I Am,—
And view the wonders of His Grace
Reflected from the Glory-Lamb.
They who had bitter tears to weep,
Have washed their robes for this great feast,
Come up through tribulation deep,
Prophet, Evangelist, and Priest,
Or ancient Bard, and Saints who long
Ago Redemption's blessed song
Discoursed in Heaven, around the Fount,
And by the Stream of Life, the Mount
Of Zion and the lofty towers
Of New Jerusalem,—bowers
Luxuriant changeful to the Light,
Fairer than Eden, and more bright.

And what a Congregation this!
So great, of men redeemed by grace.

In this unmeasured world of bliss,
Caught up from every tribe and race!
Ten thousand times ten thousand there—
From nation, people, kindred, tongue,
And thousands infinite who share
The palm, the crown, the harp well strung
To melodies; who touch the keys
Of the Seraphic harmonies;
The glad new song triumphant sing,
Hard pressing on angelic wing,
In flight supernal near the throne,
To Him the Knowing—yet Unknown.

With Him to enter into life
What joy! while from His table fed,
While to this gushing Fountain led,
With this vast world of spirits rife
With beauty, evermore to dwell
In this all glorious Capitol!

City of New Jerusalem!
Whose walls resplendent shine afar;
Twelve gates—to each a several gem,

Transfigured in each blazing star.
Whose streets are paved with finest gold
As brilliant as the Sea of Glass!
Whose gates on golden hinge unfold,
To hidden treasures that surpass
What eye hath seen, or ear hath heard,
Or yet the natural heart preferred.

The Trumpet sounds at intervals
Their welcome, who with tears and groans,
Blood sucked by tyrants on their thrones,
By king and priestly cannibals,—
Now no more curse—corroding fear-
And wiped is every rising tear.
O blessed welcome! The well done
To good and faithful Servant, Son
And heir,—enter thou into joy
Eternal of thy Honored Lord!
Thrice blessed is the soul's employ,
To execute His glorious word.

Or if on messages of love,
Or deeds of mercy, sent outside

The city limits—far above
The visible from Heaven's gate—
O what a view—so deep—so wide—
The ever varied boundless State!
The Empire of Jehovah's thought!
So vast, so complicate, sublime,
Hid in the feeblest types of time—
Where ardent towering minds are taught
In goodness infinite, and power
Supreme, to view His glory—where
No intellectual cloudlets lower.

What summits over summits rise!
The life, the love, the joy, are there!
The sons of God with eager eyes,
Delighted with the ravished throng,
Gazing on past and present long—
They linger, wonder, and adore
The Great First-Last, *whose works the more
Incline to praise*—shedding new light,
Which falls serene on radiant grove,
Or endless avenues in sight
Of Paradise; where shadows move

On field, and slope, and shining sea,
The landscapes of eternity.

There fold the curtains of the sky
O'er valleys rich with golden hue;
Afar outspread beneath the eye,
The spirit's clustering vintage grew.
How happy thus, so like the hour
Of eve inviting to repose;
Where every faculty and power
With holiest rapture glows.

NOTES.

CHAPTER I.

Catacombs.—"The name is descriptive of a subteranean excavation, and was first given in the sixth century to a limited area beneath the Church of St. Sebastian. It was afterwards generically applied to all subteranean places of sepulture." *The Catacombs of Rome*. Withrow. Page 12, note.

Appian Way.—This "Queen of Roads," as it was proudly called, was built by Appius Claudius from Rome to Brundusium; about three hundred and fifty miles in length. "This Highway, on which the Apostle Paul passed, on his way to Rome, is still lined by stately tombs in which reposed the ashes of the mighty dead, justly celebrated," says Padre Marchi, "for the extent of its cemeteries, and still more for the great number and celebrity of its Martyrs."

Dark Days.—The time of this Poem opens in the midst of the ten great persecutions of the Church, which continued until the close of the third century.

Tufa.—Volcanic rock underlying the city of Rome. It is of a greyish color, easily cut with a knife.

Gems of Art.—The grand drama, from the fall of man to the Resurrection, is here exhibited in fresco paintings from various Biblical representations. 'Ancient Art," says Dr. Lubke, "was the garment in which the young and world-agitating ideas of Christianity were compelled to veil themselves."

A Temple.—Chambers are found, adapted to this purpose, some capable of holding a small assembly of worshippers.

Sky-lit.—There were openings from above which furnished light and ventilation to the upper tier of rooms, called Luminari.

Stole.—A long, loose garment reaching to the feet.

Tonsure.—The corona or crown which priests wear as a mark of their order, and of their rank in the Church.

Nimbus.—A circle, or disk, of rays of light around the head; a halo.

One was their glorious Lord.—See Eph. iv.: 3-16. Modern controversy profanely calling in question the Divinity of Christ, never disturbed these quiet resting places. Their belief is shown in the following inscriptions: "To the One God." "God Christ Almighty." "To Christ, the One Holy God."

Praise ye the Lord.—See Ps. cxlviii.

CHAPTER II.

Martyrs.—Cyprian, in the middle of the third century, says, "It is impossible to number the martyrs of Christ." Eusebius, an eye witness of the last persecution, states that innumerable multitudes suffered during its prevalence. After describing their excruciating tortures, he adds: "And all these things were doing not for a few days, but for a series of whole years. At one time ten, or more, then twenty, again thirty or even sixty, and sometimes a hundred men, with their wives and children, were slain in one day." "We, ourselves, have seen," says the Bishop of Cæsarea, "crowds of persons, some beheaded, others burned alive, in a single day, so that the murderous weapons were blunted and broken to pieces, and the executioners, wearied with slaughter, were obliged to give over the work of blood."

Milky Way.—Was thought by the ancients to be the shining path which the gods made to Heaven.

Ignoble.—Horace, speaking of the caverns under the Esquiline hill, says: "This was the common sepulture of the miserable Plebeians."

Cæsar's Household.—The Pagan historian, Dio Cassius, says: "In the same year Domitian put to death, besides many others, Flavius Clemens, of consular dignity, though he was his cousin and married to Damilitta, who was likewise related to him. Both were charged with *Atheism.* On this ground many others, who had strayed away to the customs of the Jews (*i. e.*, converts to Christianity,) were condemned." *History of the Apostolic Church.* P. Schaff. Note 1, page 401.

Sacred Fish.—This symbol probably derived its origin from the fact that the initial letters of the names and titles of Our Lord, in Greek—Jesus Christ, Son of God, the Savior—make up the Greek word for fish. It is one of the oldest, and is found accompanying the first dated inscription which bears any emblem whatever. Withrow says: "Few symbols, if any, were more numerous than this. It occurs rudely scratched on funeral slabs, painted in the *cubicula*, sculptured on the sarcophagi, moulded on lamps, engraven on rings and seals, carved in ivory, mother-of-pearl, and precious stones, and cast in bronze or glass."

Inscriptions.—The spirit of the inscriptions and symbols is opposed to the Pagan spirit, and is almost entirely free from later Romanist errors.

Monogram.—A complex figure composed of the Greek and Roman cross combined, usually placed at the head of an inscription. It was designed to represent Christ, and was supposed to be an indication of martyrdom.

CHAPTER III.

This chapter contains the Prize Poem delivered by the author at the fourth annual Melendy prize meeting of the Alpha Kappi Phi Society of Hillsdale College, Mich., Nov. 14, 1862.

CHAPTER IV.

Arch of Titus.—Erected in commemoration of the subjugation of the Jews by Titus.

Coliseum.—An immense building, still remains; it is a third of a mile in circumference, is more than a hundred feet high and had room for 100,000 spectators.

One Victim.—Fabius, pastor of the church at Rome.

Saint Calixtus.—One of the most remarkable and most ancient areas of the Catacombs.

Martyr's Crown.—The enthusiasm for martyrdom prevailed at times, almost like an epidemic. They exulted amid their keenest pangs that they were counted worthy to suffer for their Divine Master.

CHAPTER V.

Superstition.—" The Lord brought up the vine of Christianity from a far land, and cast out the heathen, and planted and watered it, till it twined round the sceptre of the Cæsars, wreathed the columns of the Capital and filled the whole land." The heathen fanes were deserted, the gods discrowned, and the Pagan flamen no longer offered sacrifice to the Capitoline Jove. Rome, which had dragged so many conquered divinities in triumph at its chariot-wheels, at length yielded to a mightier than all the gods of Olympus." *The Catacombs of Rome*, page 117, Withrow.

CHAPTER VI.

Fossors.—Those who did the work of excavating.

Hebrew idyl.—Reference is made to Ps. xxiii.

Natal hour.—" By a noble metaphor," says Milman, " the day of their death was considered that of their birth to immortality." The church of Smyrna celebrated the anniversary of their martyred Bishop's passion, " with joy and gladness as his natal day."

Pazzolani.—A reddish, porous, friable mineral of volcanic origin.

The Cross.—On account of the abhorrence in which it was held by the Greek and Roman mind, the Christians reverently sought to veil this sign from the multitude. Hence in the earliest ages of the church there are but few representations of the cross except in some disguised form. They recognized the occurrence of this symbol everywhere in nature. It was typified in countless analogies of Scripture; in the measurement of the ark, the shape of Jacob's staff, the seven-branched candlestick, and the wave-offerings of the temple service. " This form," says Chrysostom, "at which men once shuddered, at length became the badge of highest honor, so that even emperors laid aside the diadem to assume the cross.'

CHAPTER VII.

Claudia.—A Christian woman mentioned in 2 Tim. iv.: 21, as saluting Timotheus. There is reason for supposing that this Claudia was a British maiden, daughter of King Cogidubanus, an ally of Rome, who took the name of his imperial patron, Tiberius Claudius.

The half was never told.—1 Kings. x.: 6–8.

Meditation. He is Able.—The Bible student can not fail to see in this, and in many paragraphs in the following chapters, a continual reference to Scripture.

CHAPTER VIII.

Scarlet Beast.—Rev. xvii.: 3.

Worthy.—Rev. xvi.: 6.

Latinas.—Rev. xiii.: 18. It is generally understood that this passage relates to Latinos, or the Latin kingdom.

Bow, arrows.—Ez. xxxix.: 3.

Hamonah.—Ez. xxxviii.: 16.

Widowhood.—Rev. xviii.: 7–20.

The conquering sign of Heaven.—It is said that Constantine, while marching against Maxentius, saw in the heavens a luminous cross bearing the inscription, in Greek, "Conquer by this."

Rejoice.—Rev. xix.: 3–9.

CHAPTER IX.

Mark of Beast.—Rev. xiii.: 15, 16.

A million martyrs.—It is estimated that the number of martyrs is about 50,000,000.

Janus' Temple.—At Rome, was only closed in times of universal peace.

Once more illuminated.—The figure of the cross is sometimes so arranged above Cathedral or Church spire, that it may be seen in the evening, beautifully illuminated.

CHAPTER X.

Shushan's palace.—Dan. viii.: 2; also 9 ch. 21, 23.

The Royal Princess.—Ez. xvi.: 11–14.

The Bridegroom.—Ps. xlv.: 2–8.

www.ingramcontent.com/pod-product-compliance
Lightning Source LLC
Chambersburg PA
CBHW030335170426
43202CB00010B/1136